T0067947

Words About Life

Yesterday's Memories, Today's Events, Tomorrow's Dreams

Jim Kirby

authorHOUSE®

AuthorHouse™
1663 Liberty Drive
Bloomington, IN 47403
www.authorhouse.com
Phone: 833-262-8899

© 2022 Jim Kirby. All rights reserved.

No part of this book may be reproduced, stored in a retrieval system, or transmitted by any means without the written permission of the author.

Published by AuthorHouse 03/23/2022

ISBN: 978-1-6655-5553-1 (sc)
ISBN: 978-1-6655-5561-6 (e)

Print information available on the last page.

Any people depicted in stock imagery provided by Getty Images are models, and such images are being used for illustrative purposes only. Certain stock imagery © Getty Images.

This book is printed on acid-free paper.

Because of the dynamic nature of the Internet, any web addresses or links contained in this book may have changed since publication and may no longer be valid. The views expressed in this work are solely those of the author and do not necessarily reflect the views of the publisher, and the publisher hereby disclaims any responsibility for them.

This book is dedicated to:

*My family and friends who helped me either
write or inspire to write this book.*

Mary (Alice) Nash Kirby (spouse)
Kent S. Kirby (Captain Red Beard) (Oldest son)
Kayleigh Kirby (Kent's spouse)
Ezra Nash Kirby (Grandson)
Kade A. Kirby (Mr. Mechanic) (Middle son)
Kris P. Kirby (baby boy)

Contents

A Chance I'm Taking on You

Life's to short to be alone,
And to long to be on my own,

I've been on a date or two,
But I've never met anyone like you,

Now you're going out with me,
Nothing matters now cause love is there you see,

I'm willing to take a chance on you,
I hope you will too,

We've both had some ups and downs,
Laughed at jokes and cried like sad clowns,

Yes love makes us spin round and round,
But with you I know where I'm bound,

Yes love is in me for you and I do care,
Yes together we would make a good pair,

Yes please take a chance me and you'll see,
And I believe you'll see what we can be,

Yes it's a ring and I'm asking you,
So here we are what are you going to do,

A Day Out with Dad

Kiss mom love you bye for now
I'm going out with dad cause I'm his little gal

Yes sometimes I take dad out
We go to stores and look about

We have a lot of people to see and a lot of places to go
It seems like in all the stores we go up and down ever row

A lot of things to see
No clothes or shoes for me

There's food and toys
For girls and boys

There's shoes and clothes dad says no
That's for mom to pick out when ya'll go

I ask for this and ask for that
I'm so spoiled he says I'm a brat

Sometimes he says yes sometimes he says no
When it's no I just put my hands behind my back and my eyes roll

I hang my head and stick out my lips
I wait a few seconds then lift my head with my hands now on my hips

To see if he looking my eyes are watery mom says it will work every time
Now he's looking at me and starts to mime

Then he says yes but don't tell mom
We go get this and that I got him in my palm

We go get ice cream, cookies and go to the park
Sometimes we even stay out playing till dark

Then we come home late again
Mom ask where we been?

Me and dad just smile at each other and say
It was another daughter dad day

A Few Wishes and Wants

A few wishes and wants .... for you and me,
You want this .... I wish for that,
You want to meet .... I wish I could play the blues,
You want to go out and eat .... I wish I had some new shoes,
You want to get married .... I wish it will be you,
You want to be carried .... I wish you say I do,
You want to go on a trip .... I wish to take a cruise,
You want even tip .... I wish I didn't have this bruise,
You want a girl and boy .... I wish upon a falling star,
You want happiness and joy .... I wish I had a new car,
You want to cry .... I wish to hear you sing,
You promise to never say bye .... I wish to give you a ring,

Look there's a wishing well maybe we'll get what we want.

A Little Clay A Lot of Love

A little dust a little clay,
There Adam appeared one day,

A lot of care a lot of love,
This one and only event came from Heaven above,

A perfect man from head to toe,
A pure heart and soul,

An example of what man will be,
He cared for and named all the animals on land and sea,

As time went on Adam thought there's no one for me,
He looked around and not a mate for him he could see,

God caused him to have a deep sleep,
The animals gather around without a sound or peep,

When Adam awoke he was blinded by the light,
Oh! What beauty! Oh! What a sight,

There was Eve pure, perfect as planned,
A woman and a man hand and hand,

A Little Thought A Little Prayer to My God

Lord in Heaven glory to your name
Those that have you in their heart will never be the same

But those without you there's sin and shame
And at an age of accountability have no one but themselves to blame

With you oh Lord we can shine very bright
But without you we are just wondering in the night

Thank you for being that star that shines brightest of all
Without You in this world of darkness it will be easy to stumble and fall

Thank you for all the blessings you give us
And forgive us for those time we want more and lust

So many times I have sin and fail
You have forgave me more times than I can tell

And only you can help fight off the devils strife
Only through your precious blood we have eternal life

I think about these things everyday
And I look forward and will be ready when you come get me one day

Bear in the Woods Coconut in the Tree

When it's time to let the dogs out to run around,
Bear runs for the woods with a loud barking sound,

Coconut heads for the leaning tree,
She's always chasing something she can't see,

When Bear is through in the woods chasing a cat or rabbit,
Coconut is a brown lab and she chases a ball that's a habit,

Bear doesn't to play much or chase the ball.
Coco comes running every time you call,

They act like kids, sleep like cats, and eat like hogs,
Bear and Coconut their our dogs.

Behind The Scenes

There is always someone in the church doing beyond the part,
They don't want praise, they do it from the heart,

They're only missed when somethings not done,
They don't want to be mentioned; not a credit one,

Someone has to hang the choir robes and fold the chairs,
Someone who works in the nursery and really cares,

Someone has to wash the dishes after a church meal,
To some it may not be a big deal,

It may be someone who sings next to you in the choir,
Or someone who mows the yard and never seems to tire,

I could ask, you time and time again,
Who's always working with a helping hand?

What is your part?
Are you doing it from the heart?

Bury Me Next to My Love

It seems like we have been taking care of each other for quite a while now,
We've had a lot of ups and downs, but we made it so far somehow,
Raised a few kids the best we could,
Maybe it wasn't the way others thought we should,
I wonder how many hours you spent cutting hair,
What a life, what a pair sometimes we never had a care,
Crazy things we did, and places we been,
A lot of things will probably never do again,
I think it's almost been thirty-five years now,
Times went by so fast wow!
Sometimes I wonder how many meals you have cooked for me,
How many sermons the Lord has allowed me to preach free,
I love to hear you sing,
There on your hand I see the ring,
I love you Jesus loves you,
When you're gone what will I do?
I carry you here I carry you over there,
I pace the floor over here and it seems everywhere,
What do you need babe? No I don't mind,
You've always been so kind,
I wish I could have and would have done more,
No honey you're not a bore,
Lord please take her spirit and not let me worry,
Oh! I love you Sherry.

Chasing The Wind

Don't try catching me said the wind,
I'm already up the hill and over the bend,
Besides you can't even see me,
Well maybe when I blew the leaves out of the tree,
Look I blew your kite up in the air,
You're just going to set there and stare,
So where did you go to,
Oh there you are I'm to fast for you,
I just took that hat right off the man's head,
I'm so cold today I'll make your nose red,
Today the snow is coming down,
I will blow it in your hair and all over the ground,
So go fly your kite and wear your fancy hat,
I will make the loose boards and tin go rat tat tat,
As I break the string kiss your balloons goodbye,
Watch me blow them so high,
So if you think you can catch me think again,
You can chase all day all night, but you will never catch me said the wind.

Creepy Crawly Little Things

There's always a creepy crawly little things somewhere
In the garden there's worms, doddle, and lady bugs there
In the trees there's a locust and even a raven singing
Spider webs that are full of bugs clinging
In the bathroom where those little worms or caterpillars hide
In the bedroom where the bedbugs hide
In the creek where a mosquito lands on my cheek
A June bugs in my shoes now another pair I have to seek
The bat swoops down I hit for the ground
The owl makes that hooting sound
So whats a creepy crawly thing your scared of?

Deer is on My Dear's Mind

(SHE'S HOOKED NOW)

The snow started falling heavy late one day,
There she stood gazing out the cabin door her mind so, so far away,

We had just hiked up the hill,
All the time she was thinking about a deer her first kill,

I've got a fire started and fixing a bite,
Don't think she will sleep a wink all night,

She was up two hours early and has coffee on,
Surely with all that noise and smell the deer have gone,

A little after dawn we followed the trail to our stand,
Looking around listening for a sound rifle gripped in her hand,

As we climbed up the stand and finally got settled in,
The look of nervous eyes and shaking hands I will never get to hunt again,

We took a look around with the binoculars and there was on right down
in front us,
I had to grab her arm and said. What's the rush?

She took the rifle aimed and killed her first deer,
She seemed to like that rush and kissed me right there,

I took the rifle and we climbed down,
Packed up our things and deer headed back to town,

Wait a minute I said What about my deer dear,
She said oh ok we can share my deer that made it clear,

She's hooked now,
But that's ok she's my gal,

Dedicated To My Friend And His Wife(Jamie And Jennifer Cato)
BUDDY!!!!!

Does The Blood Line Ends Here?

I've met a lot of people in my life,
Who has never had a husband or wife,
They have no children and want to be alone,
There's so many things in this world to do own your own,
Maybe some can't have kids I know this for a fact,
And for some couples (my oldest son and his wife) this is a set back,
But for now they can foster or adopt a child or two,
Some are still trying to grow up and don't want to share,
Some are happy being alone and don't care,
A few generations before me they had big families you see,
I had brothers and sisters to play and share with me,
Some families had only girls and no one is to blame,
Others had boys to carry on the family name,
So if your blood line ends here,
Just be happy and take care,

Don't Leave that Way Again

(FORGIVE ME)

Don't get mad and leave that way,
I know I'm wrong again this time this day,

Please look at me with your beautiful smile'
Since we have been together for quite a while,

You know me I know you,
Yes I've been late I time or two,

I've just been out with the boys,
Playing with our fast toys,

It seems you're a little jealous or even mad,
Oh! You're so spoiled and a face so sad,

You know you're the only one I love,
I'm being watched by one above,

Sometimes I get frustrated with you,
And I just want to walk away too,

But before I make you feel that way again,
Lets talk about what's wrong and stay together to the end,

Down to My Last Dime

What shall I do?
Where shall I go and ask who?
I'm down to my last dime,
We have to eat, don't need to steal or comment a crime,
Seems like we were just laughing and the kids were playing,
Ten years working and now we don't have anything,
Singing and praising the Lord,
Why is life so hard?
Beautiful smiles and laughs of joy,
What do I say to our little girl and boy,
Something I must have done in the past to deserve this,
Now I'm standing in a food line getting wet from the mist,
Now we have a little food to eat,
A little can goods a little meat,
It's my last dime,
And now the rents due I'm out of time,
Give up my pride and go to work at a fast food place,
All we can do is pray and say grace,
It's my last dime,
Maybe I can get a lemon or lime,
Cheer up my brother said a customer that came through,
Don't forget Jesus loves you and here's a couple hundred to help you,

Facts of Life

I heard a preacher friend of mine once say
No matter how rich or poor either way
We all will get sick or eventually die
If someone thinks that's not true that's a lie
We've all lost a family member or friend
And we know that our bodies will be in the grave in the end
Something will get us this cancer, this deadly virus and even a bad heart
We're all just here on this earth trying to do our part
Go to the doctor get another pill
Some pray for God's will
Here today gone tomorrow something about that saying
I'll just try to enjoy life till my times up set here praying

Family

You would think everyone has one,
A father, mother, a daughter, or even a son,
Some families have a few, some a lot,
I have a family to love, but some may not,
I know a few people who have no one that seem to care,
Some families are close some are hard to bear,
Some love each other, some never speak,
Some are strong some are weak,
Jealously and pride could be a few reasons,
Why families only see each other during holiday seasons,
Mom is still here dad is gone,
We have three boys of our own,
They will soon grow up and move away,
So love and cherish your family before they are gone one day,
Stick and stay together,
Love and be happy forever,

Ghosts of The Old House

Midnight the clock just struck twelve o'clock,
Every night about this time it could be heard around the block,
The old two story house has been empty for years,
The couple that lived there died and no one even cares,
Sometimes there's a light in the attic yellow and bright,
No one dares to go there especially at night,
One cool Halloween night while some kids were passing by,
A big old owl and a few bats were flying in the night sky,
The owl dove down over the kids got them turned around,
They were so dazed and scared they couldn't make a sound,
After a few minutes they decide to move slowly away,
Wind blew and slammed the door, the kids ran they weren't about to stay,
Once again the ghost laughed and said we are safe for now,
The old house also was guarded by a wolf with a loud growl,
And while on a broom followed by the owl and a few bats,
There was another ghost who loves to scare,
Those who come by the old house wither by challenge or dare,
There's your warning from the ghost of the old house,

Haircuts

Yes I needed a haircut yesterday,
Maybe I will have time today,
Or after I finish listening to my favorite song,
My hairs over my ears and getting to long,
If not today, tomorrow will always be an option for me,
Appointment for some, but I'm a walk in you see,
Some peoples hair grows fast, while others grow slow,
Set up straight, cut, buzz or a trim off your hair will go,
I remember when I was a lad,
Going to the barber with my dad,
I think a haircut was a dollar fifty then,
We want ever see that again,
From a trim to a buzz,
Those with a beard or even a little peach fuzz,
From the bangs NO! NO! not the curls,
No not the one on the pretty little girls,
Some dye their hair, some get a perm,
Some wiggle and squirm,
Yes I needed a haircut yesterday,
Maybe I will have time today,

Heaven

There is a place I hear about called Heaven,
Where everything is perfect, even the number seven,

This place has an eternal flow of milk and honey,
So there will be no need of food or money,

We'll have mansion and walk on streets of gold,
Where no one will get lonely, or grow old,

Just to praise Jesus all day long,
And where we will never get tired of singing the same song,

I've tasted the honey straight from the comb,
And now heaven will be my next home,

Heavens not just another place somewhere above,
But a place of eternal happiness and love,

A place where My Father, and My Savior de well,
And when you take a drink of that everlasting water you will never fear hell,

You have a choice to be saved, a new life born again,
To go to Heaven where life will never end,

It's Not Natural (Always Being The Best)

It's not natural to be this good,
I was always the fastest in the neighborhood,

I could hit that ball so far with that piece of wood,
As small as I was no one thought I could,

I threw that football so far,
It went past that speeding car,

I swung so hard the ball flew off the tee,
There it goes over that tall pine tree,

The ball was passed to me,
I kicked it so hard and fast the goalie couldn't even see,

I picked up the weight carried up the hill,
I won because no one else had that kind of will,

I'm in the ring moving so fast,
My one two hit you with a blast,

I'm setting in a game of chess,
One wrong move now I'm the best,

Now I'm in a game of pool,
Don't try to hustle me I'm a natural not a fool,

The ball is bounce to me and it seems like every time I shoot it goes in,
Where ever I go I end up being a winner in the end,

Gliding like a graceful ice skater twirling in the air,
With a perfect score, it doesn't seem fair,

As I bounce off the board with twist, turns, and hit the water,
The next one up shouldn't even bother,

With the stick in my hand, and the puck on the ice,
The goalie better hide and look for some advice,

So in any sport you play, whether your woman are man,
Always do the best you can,

Just A Little Time (A Child Ask)

Spending a few minutes, a few hours, out with me to play,
Just a little time goes a long way,

It may only be for a little while,
But it will bring a smile,

Playing in the mud playing in the rain,
Stop and listen here comes the train,

Sometimes you come to school and have lunch with me,
It's just a few things here and there you see,

When we play a game it seems like I always win,
This seems to happen time and time again,

I know you have to work a lot,
But why I have a lot,

But it seems you always make on my birthdays,
You have time for me on all those holidays,

So thanks for just a little time you've always had,
Love you mom and dad.

Just to Get Away

There's something I got to do,
It has to be done and seen through,

I need to get far, far, away,
Not next week or tomorrow but today,

Leave all my family, work, and even my phone,
Pack my back pack and I'm gone,

I can't get there fast enough,
It will be a long and maybe rough,

As I catch a ride to the edge of the woods,
All I have is my back pack with all my goods,

I'll hike up the mountain for a few hours
This place is nice and thanks to a friend of ours

Now there's the cabin in the middle of nowhere,
Cooking on an open fire and not having to share,

Two weeks of my life each year,
I'm crawling up in a chair with a good book and not a care,

Things I will do and see,
Looking all over this land with ah standing next to this tall tree,

I never want to leave here I'm free,
Just to get away Jesus, the mountains and me.

Dedicated To My friend Jeremy Smallwood

Laugh Smile Enjoy Life

I know there is things that come our way in life
Good things bad things happiness and strife
Some of us smile and laugh to keep going each day
But when we are sick or have a lost a love one what can we say?
It's hard sometimes to be happy and laughing all the way
Yes it's hard sometimes not to get down and keep the negativity away
I know some people despite their ups and downs
Seem to always be laughing and smiling circus clowns
People say what's in your and mind
Will eventually come out wither kind or mean
Laugh even tell a few jokes make someone else smile
Someone may ask you what makes life worth while
Then you can tell them Jesus is the reason
All year around and not just for a season
Try to make every situation a happy one
When something goes wrong don't give up and be done
Live smile enjoy each moment of life
Yes we can make it with smiles through this worlds strife
One for you one for me
Laugh smile and happy you will be

Life is Life

Life is full of surprises,
Surprises we still don't expect,
Expect them though because they will sneak up on you,
You really have to be ready for anything,
Anything everything from being late to work,
Work so we can pay bills and eat,
Eat so we keep up with what life brings us each day,
Day to day and night to night,
Night where so of us work and others try to sleep,
Sleep to get our rest for our busy lives,
Lives where we have expected anything to go wrong,
Wrong is wrong and right is right,
Right we think we always are as men,
Men who are aren't always right ask a woman,
Woman named Alice I live each day of my life,
Life is life,

Life is Like A Long Dream

Life is like a long dream
A dream we live everyday
A dream that seems to last forever for some
Sometimes life is full of happiness and gleam
Other times in life we have sadness as we grow older and gray
But life doesn't always have to be like a sour plum

Life is like a long dream
And for those who have slowed down and run out of steam
We lay and put to rest
And they go to a place for them that is best
None of us go west or east
From those of greatness to the least
We either go up or down
It's up to the sky or down below the ground
The saved go to finally meet their Master
The lost or on their way to disaster

Life is like a long dream
A dream that will last until I see my Savior one day
Jesus will meet and lead the saved to that anticipated land of milk and honey
Oh! Heaven and to cross that beautiful crystal stream
And there we will hear our Master's voice say
Come my faithful servants stay with me where it will never be dark but always sunny
We all will sang and rejoice
And will tire of your voice

Lonely Rose

There she stands alone above all
So beautiful, lean, and tall
She is in plain sight
Even in the dark she shines bright
But yet she is lonely rose
She has a beautiful smile big eyes and a little nose
Why is she so lonely and sad?
Some say it's because of her many colors she once had
Red as a Valentine's Heart
Yellow as the sun when the clouds part
White as a sheet
Pink as the heart when two lover's meet
Beautiful as she is why so alone
Why have all the other flowers left and gone
Ah! Here comes a hand to help her up down
She is put in a vase
She will put a smile on a woman's face
If for a day a week or so
She want be lonely where ever she may go

Mary and Our Three Little Lambs

I just knew one day I would marry
And through the door her I would carry

We had three boys
A lot of diapers a lot of toys

They set up crawl and now run
Oh! What a lot of fun

Blonde hair a little curls and big blue eyes
Almost the color of the summer skies

Sometimes they smile and laugh and even cry
Oh! Lord how we try

One on the house always being curious
We would get scared then furious

Oh no hit the pole stitches on the head
It's been a long day time for bed

Two surgeries last year of school
That's not really cool

They were all in the band
They've been all over the state even went to another land

One day they may marry
And a grand baby we may carry

Mary oh Mary
Why are they so contrary?

Look like me act like you
Oh! What are we going to do?

LOVE YOU ALL MARY ALICE KENT (KAYLIEGH KENT'S WIFE)
KADE KRIS OH (EZRA OUR GRANSON) AND SHAYLA TOO

Mom Says...

Moms always saying things like I need this I need that,
Today I need some shoes tomorrow I need a hat,

Mom says clean your room,
Here's a dust pan and a broom,

Mom says wash your hands time to eat,
Be good eat all on your plate and get a treat,

Mom says brush your teeth comb your hair,
I think is anyone really going to care,

Mom says we are going to the store,
She has a list food shoes and more,

Mom says what color shoes do I want to wear,
I can't make up my mind she's about to pull out her hair,

Mom says red ones blue ones pick one now,
I close my eyes and point at the brown ones somehow,

Mom says get them your just like your dad can't make up your mind,
Well mom thinks for saying that dad thanks your kind,

What? Mom's has nothing to say,
Hum? I wonder how long she will stay this way,

My Best Friend

You are my best friend,
And I know our friendship will never end,

Even though we are many miles apart,
We are still best friends in our hearts,

You are the best friend anyone can ask for,
You would do all you could for me and then more,

And if I needed a helping hand,
I would call and there you would stand,

Your not just another friend,
Your there time and time again,

I sent you a letter,
Just wishing we were together,

But now you've moved and gone,
I just sit here on my own,

And when our lives end,
We'll still be friends,

My Prayer

This is my prayer at night
It doesn't seem to be much

But I say it with all my heart
I try not to leave out any part

Heavenly Father up above
I'm thankful for your love

I ask you to help the sick, poor, and old
That with you they will never be lonely or cold

And you said you would forgive of my sin
And help me to never do it again

Thank you for all my food
Oh Lord when things go wrong help my stay in a good mood

Lead me, guide me, and direct me in your will
I ask you for your protection from those who kill

Lord if it's your will please let the girl of my life
One day be my wife

I ask all these things in Your precious name
Without one word of shame

Old Hickory

I've had this old cane for a long time,
It was my grandpa's, then my dad's back when things cost a dime,

Dad said that (OLD HICKORY) was engraved on the side,
He thinks it was just before his grandpa had died,

OLD HICKORY is a good name, and a good piece of wood,
I wouldn't sell it even if I could,

OLD HICKORY and I have been through a lot together,
When it is cold, hot, and all kinds of weather,

Sometimes it helps me up it helps me down,
It helps me up when I get dizzy and start to spin round and round,

When I go for a walk in the park,
Here comes that dog and his bark,

I grip it tight and use it to lean on,
The dog thinks it's his bone,

It seems that me and OLD HICKORY are closer that a brother,
Sometimes it feels heavy other times it's light as a feather,

Do I really need this cane?
Yes I do don't be so vain,

I guess one day when I die and lay OLD HICKORY down,
Someone will pick it up, why worry I want be around,

Our Time is Melting Away

Our time is melting away,
What are we doing about each day?
Our lives seem to be going by so fast,
Slow down it doesn't hurt once in a while to be last.
Up at four-thirty and out the door,
I'm off to work to make more money more, more,
Seems like I was just a kid a few years ago,
Time is melting so fast. Where did it go?
Just a few turn arounds of life and some time is gone,
A house, a wife, and three boys that's my own,
Life's going so fast, like ice cream melting in the sun,
I need to slow down with my family and have some fun,
Slow down like molasses on a cold winters day,
What have I done? What do I have to say?
Kids are over with grand kids and they want to play,
Oh! I miss them so much wish they could stay,
I can't go back to the past and change anything,
I just need to slow down and listen to the birds sing.

Please Keep Me (Mom-Dad)

How did I get here accidentally or willing? .... Please don't abort me that will be killing,

Whatever the situation was please don't let me go .... Yes I do have a soul,

Whatever the situation is keep me please ..... One day I will smile and even sneeze,

Whatever the situation will be .... I will love you so please love me,

OH! MOM OH! DAD I don't ever want you to say .... Where's my baby at today,

See how beautiful I am .... Mary I'm your little lamb,

Just imagine one day my laugh my smile .... One day we could play ball,

Oh please keep me .... Maybe I'll have blue, brown, or green eyes you see,

I love you hope you love me .... I will laugh one day when you say Wee! Wee!

I don't know the past .... But I hope our relationship will last,

I don't know my future here .... But if not with you maybe someone somewhere,

I'm here in your belly with you .... Keep me and you would be blue,

Please don't give me up .... I'm not a cat or pup,

Please don't let me go .... NO! NO! NO!

Please don't let them take me away .... You know I want to stay,

You just found out I'm a few weeks old .... If you keep me you will see I'm more precious than gold,

I want you to keep me warm .... I don't want to be alone and cold.......

(Pride) Please Don't Bring Me Down

Some say I'm pretty good at what I do,
It's not up to me to say but who?

A word of advice to those who brag on themselves,
Pride will bring you down by yourselves,

Some say I'm good maybe the best,
But there's need for me to brag or stick out my chest,

Sometimes I have to stop and get away,
Don't need to listen what people say,

In any sport even the game of life,
People will say things that will cut like a knife,

Rise to the top is great,
Fall to the bottom people will hate,

So please don't put me on a pedestal on top,
Because one day I will fall and pop

Do your best at what you do,
Even if you are sky high, or down and blue,

Remember someone is always watching you,
Your family, kids, and even Jesus too,

Rumble Stumble Tumble

When I was a boy,
We were so poor and hardly ever got a toy,

So we had to find other things to do,
I would chase someone then they would chase me too,

Sometimes we would go a roadside park,
There we would find a hill and roll down and it would leave a mark,

Rumble stumble tumble down the hill we would roll,
After several times up and down we had plenty of bruises to show,

A scrape here a scrape there,
We would even get in a tire and roll down without a care,

Dirt in our hair holes in our clothes red in the face,
But still this was our favorite place,

Rumble stumble tumble down the hill,
Oh! What a thrill,

The Chase

I'll stop chasing her the day she says I do
But I haven't ask her yet I'm not through

Oh! She's the dream of my life
And I'll chase that beauty queen till she's my wife

My friends and even my dad said
Let her chase you till she's mad

But they don't see what I see
Those big blue eyes staring at me

They just memorize me in my track
That long curly blonde hair running down her back

There she goes again
Wonder when the chase will end

Where did she go?
Well guess I'll look and then low

I think I lost her for now
But the chase is still on I'll find her somehow

I heard she was chasing me
Now it's my time you see

This chase is fun
But it's about I stop being on the run

I let her catch me always let her win
That way she'll always come back again and again

The Goat Who Acted Like A Dog

Someone once gave me a goat named Billy,
He didn't act like a goat, but acted quite silly,

As soon as they opened the gate he ran straight for the dog food,
I heard a goat would eat about anything, but to the dogs this was rude,

So there he was baa-ing, baa-ing and eating away,
He was everywhere, in the shed, in the garden this went on all day,

He started chasing the hens, and jumping on the car. THAT WAS IT!!
I built a pen and locked him in, of course, he threw a fit,

A few days had passed, he finally settled down,
I let him out to play, he started acting strange running round and round,

The dogs left for their morning walk, and he wanted to go,
He started to baa-ing, again and tried to leave. I SAID NO!!

The dogs were about out of site, he jumped the fence and off he went,
As he looked around smelling with his nose to the ground looking for a
scent,

He's got their scent off he went jumping over a log,
There goes Billy acted like a dog,

Silly old goat named Billy,
Who wants to be a dog, how silly,

The Gold Fish that Lived in A Well

There once was goldfish that lived in a well,
How he got there is no tall tale,
A boy named Ezra bought a goldfish at the pet store,
That's all he could get because he was poor,
He took the goldfish home put him in a bowl gave him a name,
He named him Orange and he was very easy to tame,
Sometimes he would Orange out to play,
Then something happened on day,
When Ezra reach down to tie his shoe,
He looked up a bird got orange and off he flew,
Ezra chased him as far as he could,
The bird landed on a well made of brick and wood,
The bird dropped Orange and he went down the well,
Ezra looked all around and there was a rope and pail,
He lowered the pail down but couldn't get him out,
Jump in Ezra said with a loud shout,
Here you will have to stay,
Don't worry I will come see you and bring you food everyday,
So upon that hill,
There lives a goldfish named Orange who lives in a well,

Dedicated to Ezra Nash Kirby (our grandson)

Three Kites are Waiting

Mom and dad seem to be too busy for me,
But I heard them talking and that's going to change you see,

Hi! I'm Shayla I'm seven years old,
Spending time with my mom and dad is more precious than gold,

One day after their work they're going to take me to the store,
They said just one toy only, cause I think we are poor,

Up and down every isle we go no toys or dolls
No board games puzzles or balls,

There they are just what I been looking for,
They just have three left in a box by the door,

The three kites one for me one for mom and one for dad,
They both look at me one looked shocked the other sad,

They both said ok dear you can have all three,
I was so happy the three kites mom dad and me,

To A Girl I Love

There is a girl I love
She is purer than I white dove

But she is so far away
All I do is think about her all day

I wish she was with me
So we could discuss what we want to be

She is the dream of my life
Oh I hope and pray she will be my wife

She is still young now
But I will wait on her somehow

I love her with all my heart as a close friend
And I hope that our friendship will never end

I send her letters because I can't be there
But life isn't always fair

So one day I hope the wait will be worth while
When we walk down the isle

And I hope with all my heart
That it is her beside me saying her part

To Be Free

To be free,
Free as a bird from a cage,
Cage of a life,
Life that we live everyday,
Everyday we get trapped in this world you see,
See me wanting to get free,
Free so free flying away,
Away to be alone,
Alone and have time to do some thinking,
Thinking about you, me and life,
Life to be free,
Free as the wind,
Wind from all directions,
Directions I need to follow,
Follow so I don't get trapped again,
Again not to mess up and sin,
Sin that only Jesus can take away,
Away to Heaven and be free.

Todays Events

Today's planned events are happening now it's here
So do the right thing today so there want be any regrets for yesterday
Live for today take it easy and slow
Everything you do today will become yesterdays memory somehow somewhere
Be happy have fun enjoy the time of this day
Today is up to you no matter what you do or where you go

We are not promised tomorrow that's life
And life's not fair
So smile and say kind words as you are passing by
We all have good or bad things going on in this world of strife
So today as we go think about what we can share
Again smile, love, and just try

Tomorrows Dreams

Yesterday is gone,
Today is here,
Will tomorrow ever come?
Tomorrows dreams can be shown,
We have plenty of dreams we can share,
Everyone has some,
When we doze off or fall asleep and dream away,
Our minds wonder here and there,
Even though tomorrows not here we still dream it,
I'll do it tomorrow is a frequent saying I here today,
I should have done that or this but something stops us like a fear,
Leave a memory for yesterday, dream today, and don't quit,

Trash

Trash, trash, trash, it is everywhere,
Garbage, bottles, a lot of paper, and even a tuna can,
Old clothes, shoes with holes, and even a to go tray,
I put my all my trash in a big bag or can and set it curb side.
Loud noise from a trash truck passing by,

Mash, mash, mash, oh what do I hear,
The familiar sound of a truck, run by man,
Up and down scraps of paper blowing and land where it may,
OH! MY so much garbage, so much trash I almost cried,
What can I do to stop this world of trash that's become a pigs sty?

Flash, flash, flash, the trash is piling up in flash,
The trash is taken to a place and piled so high,
Setting in the park watching the wind blow trash right by me,
Trash in the grass, trash on the road,
Trash on the beach, trash in the sea,
Will anyone help me with this trash?

Cash, cash, cash, recycle get some cash,
Some people don't even care or try,
Recycle and save another tree,
So arrogant so bold,
We can do this together and make this a better place to be,
Think before you throw down your trash,

TRASH TRASH TRASH

What will A Man Do for A Dime?

In this day and time,
A man will do just about anything for a dime,

He will leave his wife, kids, and sell his home,
Just to get his way or something of his own,

He will lie, cheat, and steal,
To fulfill a habit, or get a thrill,

He will look back one day,
And say I wish I hadn't gambled it all away,

He will sell his truck or car,
To get a drink or go to a bar,

And a man that uses, buys, and sells dope,
There will never be any hope,

So I ask you? If a man will do all this for a dime?
What will he do for a dollar in time,

What You Going To Do Now?

(A SECOND CHANCE)

What you going to do now?
You got me to smile somehow

You got me to talking I said hi
That's hard to do I'm very shy

Now you're holding my hand
We are just looking at the sea and walking in the sand

Your smile is working on my heart
You're off to a good start

Your eyes are glowing
My hands are sweating

My heart is starting to pound
Now you're standing there without a sound

We've both been hurt before
And our hearts have been tore

Maybe this is a chance to start over again
And not worry about where we've been

Oh! Another date
Oh! That's great
Oh! Another week
Oh! A kiss on the cheek
Oh! It's been a year
Oh! You want to be my dear
Oh! A ring
Oh! Let the wedding bells ring

WHAT YOU GOING TO DO NOW?

Whistling Cool Breeze

One cold winters night there by the fire
A man set in his chair in his bedtime attire
A cup of coco, a piece of bread, and some cheese
As he started to eat he shivered as he felt a breeze
He raised up looked all around the house
There was something stirring and it was a mouse
As the clock struck eight with a loud tone
The mouse climbed up in his little chair with his bedtime attire on
A little cheese, bread, and some coco for me
Thank you said the mouse that's why I like you, you see
As the mouse reach for the cheese
The man started to sneeze
The man started to stare
The cool breeze made the fire have a bright glare
The man's eyes dead set on me even more
Oh! Said the mouse I forgot something maybe the door
So the mouse climbed down and jumped from his chair
On his way over to the door he could feel the chill in the air
Now the door was shut and no more chill
Now they could be warm and eat their meal

Why Are You Mine?

You're looking at me,
I wonder what you see,
Maybe you're thinking? Why are you mine?
How did I pick you up? What was that line?
Anyhow you fell for it line, hook, sinker and all,
I don't know what you saw,
I seen a loving beautiful gal,
Who I hope to be my best pal,
Looking at that curly hair and hazel eyes,
All hellos and never any goodbyes,
When you give me that wink,
My heart begins to sink,
Why are you mine?
Cause your heart is big and your so fine,
You've been mine for some time now,
I've been yours and we've stayed together some how,
Why are you mine I ask again,
Because your more than my friend,

Yesterday's Memories

Yesterday is gone, gone, gone
So it's best to leave it alone
Yes it is true we can learn from things of yesterday
Some good things and some bad things but don't let them dwell too long
today
Yes we can cherish a picture of a love one or friend
Some of those memories will be with us till the end
There isn't one thing we can go back and do again
I would have or I should or I could have done
There's not one minute, day, week, month, or even a year no not one
Many times I would say if only I have done this or went here
Maybe been this or started that I may have something to share
If you worry too much it could bring you down
Even lead to bad health and under the ground
Yes I remember when is a good start to a conversation
But just remember don't let you down or control your destination
See and talk to all your family and that best friend
So one day they will be a happy memory in the end

You and Me

One and a two,
You know I love you,

Three and a four,
You're the only one I adore,

Five and six,
We always seem to stick together when we get in a fix,

Seven and an eight,
I will always love and never hate,

Nine and a ten,
Love you always not just now and then,

Printed in the United States
by Baker & Taylor Publisher Services